THE SCIENCE
OF A
FLIP TURN

TAMRA B. ORR

Published in the United States of America by Cherry Lake Publishing
Ann Arbor, Michigan
www.cherrylakepublishing.com

Content Adviser: Michael Giromini, Director of Regional School Improvement and Accountability at Plymouth-Canton
Community Schools, former physics teacher and swim coach
Reading Adviser: Marla Conn, ReadAbility, Inc.

Photo Credits: © Dennis Sabo/Shutterstock Images, cover, 1; © SUSAN LEGGETT/Shutterstock.com, 5; © Staff/MCT/
Newscom, 6; © technotr/iStockphoto, 7; © BananaStock/Thinkstock Images, 8; ©Gert Very/Shutterstock Images, 11;
© Solis Images/Shutterstock Images, 13, 17, 22; © amriphoto/iStock Images, 15; © Randolph Jay Braun/Thinkstock
Images, 19; © Dennis Sabo/Shutterstock Images, 21; © Mitchell Gunn/Dreamstime.com, 24; © tunart/iStockphoto, 26;
© Brian McEntire/iStockphoto, 28

Library of Congress Cataloging-in-Publication Data

Orr, Tamra
 The science of a flip turn/Tamra B. Orr.
   pages cm.—(Full-Speed Sports)
 Includes index.
 Audience: Age: 8–12.
 Audience: Grade: 4 to 6.
 ISBN 978-1-63362-583-9 (hardcover)—ISBN (invalid) 978-1-63362-763-5 (pdf)—ISBN 978-1-63362-673-7 (paperback)—
ISBN 978-1-63362-853-3 (ebook)
 1. Swimming—Starts and turns. I. Title.

GV838.53.S75O77 2015
797.2—dc23
                    2014050351

Cherry Lake Publishing would like to acknowledge the work of
the Partnership for 21st Century Skills. Please visit *www.p21.org*
for more information.

Printed in the United States of America
Corporate Graphics

ABOUT THE AUTHOR

Tamra B. Orr is the author of more than 400 books for readers of all ages. Tamra, who has four
grown kids, lives in the Pacific Northwest with her husband, dog, and cat. She is a graduate of Ball
State University and spends most of her free time reading, camping, and finding out more about
the world around her.

TABLE OF CONTENTS

CHAPTER 1

WHOSE IDEA WAS THIS?

Have you ever watched what competitive swimmers in a race do when they reach one end of the pool? They turn a quick **somersault**, push off the wall with their feet, and head in the opposite direction. This is more than just a slick move: the flip turn is, without question, a speedy, **efficient** way to help an athlete win a race.

Several people claim the honor of coming up with the flip turn—or at least putting it to use in a swimming competition. History, however, hasn't quite decided who to credit.

In the mid-1940s, All-American swimming champion Dorothy "Dottie" Schwartz became the first woman to use a flip turn in a race. At the age of 19, she was standing on the starting block in Louisville, Kentucky, ready for the 100-yard freestyle women's race in the National Amateur Athletic Union competition. The signal to start went off, and the swimmers hit the water. One minute, 5.5 seconds later, Schwartz was the winner, thanks in part to those flip turns.

Young swimmers learn flip turns so they can turn around faster.

Al VandeWeghe was one of the first swimmers to experiment with the flip turn.

SWIMMING
Streamlining the body

Fractions of a second can decide a race, so well-executed turns are key.

Flip turn
Freestyle*

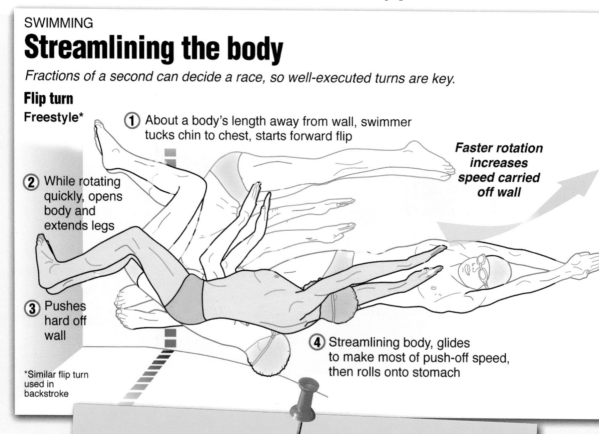

① About a body's length away from wall, swimmer tucks chin to chest, starts forward flip

Faster rotation increases speed carried off wall

② While rotating quickly, opens body and extends legs

③ Pushes hard off wall

④ Streamlining body, glides to make most of push-off speed, then rolls onto stomach

*Similar flip turn used in backstroke

LOOK!

A well-done flip turn looks like a kind of underwater acrobatics. Study this diagram. What other activities do these movements remind you of? Can you see any of them used in gymnastics? How about martial arts or maybe dancing?

A flip turn is similar to a somersault.

Swimmer Al VandeWeghe, silver medal winner at the 1936 Olympics, is one person who claimed credit for the flip turn. As a teenager, he wanted to improve his speed. "Back in those days, you had to touch the wall before you turned, and my legs were pretty heavy," he stated in a 1987 interview. "I had a real slow **conventional** turn. One day I was experimenting and tried this new turn by flipping over on my side and kicking off the end of the pool."

Many experts believe the flip turn inventor was Julian "Tex" Robertson, a man who has coached generations of

Flip turns can be difficult for young swimmers.

swimmers. One of his many students was Adolph Kiefer, who was competing in the backstroke at the 1936 Summer Olympics. Robertson showed him a special turn—the flip turn. It helped Kiefer win the gold medal.

No matter who invented it, the flip turn is one of the most commonly used moves in swim races—from those at the local community pool to Olympic competitions. It saves time and smoothly gets the swimmer from one lap to the next.

CHAPTER 2

On Your Mark, Get Set...

If you have ever tried swimming laps, you probably know how confusing it can be when you reach one end of the pool. What do you do now? Swimming up to the wall, touching it with your hands, and then turning around, planting your feet against the side, and pushing off feels awkward. It also slows you down.

Professional swimmers—who know that every fraction of a second means the difference between winning and losing a race—struggle with this problem, too. The flip turn makes the transition between laps much easier, but the turn is not always easy to learn. It requires breathing, turning, and pushing with just the right timing.

When to start the flip turn is one challenge swimmers encounter. If they start it too far away from the wall, their feet will barely brush the wall or miss it completely. They will not be able to push off. On the

Sometimes, the swimmer with the best flip turn wins the race.

Lines on the bottom of the pool can help a swimmer judge the distance to the wall.

other hand, if they start it too close, they run the risk of hitting their heads or feet on the hard wall or not being able to plant their feet the way they wanted.

The answer awaited on the floor of the pool. If you've ever gone swimming in a lap pool, you may have noticed the black lines painted on the bottom. Those lines are there to make sure swimmers don't stray out of the lanes and bump into other swimmers.

If you look closer, however, you will notice that at the end of each of those lines is a short horizontal line. This shorter line tells the swimmer the wall is just 2 feet (0.6 meters) away and it's time to start that flip turn.

But how is the flip turn done, and what does science have to do with it?

THINK ABOUT IT!

Doing a flip turn on the side of the pool is very similar to doing a squat jump on land. The position of the feet, the push of the legs, and the muscles used are almost the same. How could practicing squats at home help a swimmer do stronger flip turns in the water?

— CHAPTER 3 —

GOING AGAINST INSTINCT

One of the most important pieces of advice any coach will tell swimmers is to *not* slow down as they approach the wall. In fact, they are supposed to speed up! This is tough, because basic human instinct tells you to do the opposite. "Danger straight ahead!" an inner voice screams. "Impact is imminent! Slow down, slow down before you slam into the wall!" Ignoring that voice isn't easy. Is speeding up really necessary when performing the flip turn?

According to science, the answer is yes.

Flip turns aren't the only important part of racing—
a good swimmer also knows how to time her breathing.

In swimming races, the faster you go the better. Shaving just a hundredth of a second off of your time can put you in first place or even break world records. Having a good flip turn will improve your time.

The flip turn is based on two related things: **energy** and **velocity**.

Picture yourself in the pool. You just spotted the mark on the pool floor telling you the wall is 2 feet away. You take one more quick, deep breath. Remember—the flip turn is done underwater, so you need to take in

Your legs push you off the wall.

enough air before you turn or you will run out mid-flip.
You kick extra hard to increase your speed as you
approach the wall.

At this point, all of your body's energy is going in one
direction: toward the wall. If you slow down, look at the
wall, or start your turn too early, you lose speed, which
means you lose energy (and **momentum**). That's the
last thing you want to happen.

The flip turn transfers a body's energy from one
direction to the opposite direction. In order to do this,

swimmers have to curl into a somersault position. This makes their bodies more compact, so they can maintain speed and reduce **drag**.

How do you do a somersault on the ground? Chances are, you start by tucking your chin. Swimmers do the same thing. Then they use their arms to push water behind them, transferring more momentum into the rotation of the turn.

What's next? Plant, push, and rotate!

GO DEEPER!

Have you ever studied what happens to your body when you do a somersault? Usually you do them too fast to think about it. Try doing the slowest somersault you can. What muscles do you use the most? How many steps are there between tucking, rolling, and standing back up? How would this feel different in the water?

CHAPTER 4

DOING THE BREAKOUT

When you do a somersault on the floor, you usually end up back on your feet. Swimmers who do the flip turn correctly end up with their feet on the wall.

As their feet plant firmly on the pool wall, all of the energy moving their bodies forward through the water is absorbed into the feet.

Swimmers bend their knees as soon as their feet touch the wall. This way, they can push off the balls of their feet with great power and strength. The push-off provides most of the velocity coming out of a turn. Only a little of it comes from the built-up energy the swimmer had when heading into the wall.

Swimmers come out of the flip turn facing upward. This is where **rotation** comes into the movement.

This swimmer is mid-somersault, about to touch the wall with his bent legs. Once he does, he will straighten them to push off.

This swimmer will soon rotate back onto her stomach.

While pushing off the wall, swimmers rotate their bodies so that their faces are, once again, pointed down at the bottom of the pool. Swimmers call this part of the turn the breakout.

In order to increase speed, swimmers put their arms straight out in front of them, with their hands together.

This swimmer is somersaulting towards the wall.

They squeeze their elbows together and hold their legs and back straight. Their chins remain tucked, to keep their bodies long and pointed. This lessens drag on their bodies and allows them to move faster. Think of a long, lean pencil being pushed through the water, as opposed to a wide, thick eraser.

As the energy from the push off the wall begins to slow, swimmers begin to dolphin kick. For a dolphin kick, they keep their legs close together with their knees slightly bent. They tighten their core

This swimmer has streamlined himself to swim faster.

[21ST CENTURY SKILLS LIBRARY]

muscles, and move their hips up and down. After a couple of kicks, the swimmers rotate their whole bodies so they are looking at the bottom of the pool again. As they break the surface of the water, swimmers keep their strokes close to their sides, pushing a great deal of water out of the way without changing their **streamlined** position. Now, they are back to laps, and hoping that flip turn gave them the speed they need to win first prize.

GO DEEPER!

Flip turns involve doing a somersault in the water. How do swimmers prevent water from going up their noses? Coaches teach swimmers to take a quick, deep breath before going into the turn. Then, they are taught to breathe slowly and steadily out of their noses and mouths as they make the turn. How do you think this helps?

CHAPTER 5

WITH A LITTLE HELP FROM THE FLIP TURN

Anyone who has ever seen Michael Phelps fly through the water remembers the sight. Between 2004 and 2012, this young man from Maryland earned an astounding 22 Olympic medals—18 gold, two silver, and two bronze. That many medals set another record: the most medal wins by any Olympic athlete in history.

At age 15, Phelps became the youngest American male swimmer to compete in the Olympics in almost 70 years. A few months later, he set a world swimming record in the 200-meter **butterfly**. Since then, he has continued to set records and earn medals.

One of the reasons Phelps has done so well is his skill at the flip turn. He is so flexible that during the breakout, he squeezes his elbows together behind his head, rather than against his ears. He also tucks his

As of 2015, Michael Phelps has won 22 Olympic medals.

Wearing a swim cap can help a swimmer be more streamlined, since his or her hair doesn't float around.

chin down to his chest. Both moves make him more streamlined than his competitors.

Being able to do perfect, fast, streamlined flip turns will not guarantee any swimmer a medal. It takes much more to win a swimming competition. However, knowing how to do flip turns and understanding the science behind them may help a good swimmer become a great one.

A number of products have come and gone on the market to help people learn how to do flip turns. One company created a flip turn station involving

THINK ABOUT IT!

Flip turns are only allowed in backstroke and freestyle swimming competitions. How would the approach to the wall be different when doing these types of strokes? In butterfly and breaststroke competitions, the swimmer touches the wall with both hands at the same time and then turns around. Why do you think they do it this way?

Swimming is a popular sport for young people.

underwater platforms for kids to stand on and practice.
Another company has raised the money to make the
first activity tracker for swimmers. The tracker will be
worn on the head, and keep track of the number and
speed of laps and the quality of flip turns.

In the end, however, the key to doing great flip turns
takes the same thing as anything else—practice,
practice, and more practice.

TIMELINE

A TIMELINE HISTORY OF SWIMMING

1896	Swimming is added to the first modern Olympic Games in Athens.
1908	The current governing swimming association, FINA (Fédération Internationale de Natation de Amateur), is formed.
1912	Women are allowed to swim in the Summer Olympic Games in Stockholm.
1936	Al VandeWeghe and Adolph Kiefer both use the flip turn in the Summer Olympics.
1946	Dorothy Schwartz uses the flip turn in a women's race.
1972	Mark Spitz breaks all swimming records at the Munich Olympics.
1984	In the 100 meter freestyle in the Los Angeles Olympics, Nancy Hogshead and Carrie Steinseifer (who are also roommates) touch the wall at the *exact* same time—for the first-ever tie in Olympic swimming history.
2000	Eric "the Eel" Moussambani, from Equatorial Guinea, competes in the Sydney Olympics. He qualifies thanks to a program to help countries that don't have good swimming facilities. He's only practiced swimming for a few months, and only in a lake!
2004	Ian Thorpe loses his balance and falls into the water right before a race in the Australian Championships, starting a huge controversy about if that counted as a false start, or starting the race too early.
2012	Michael Phelps wins his 22nd Olympic swimming medal at the Summer Games in London.
2015	French swimmer Camille Muffat, 25, is killed in a helicopter crash in Argentina. She had won gold, silver, and bronze medals in the London Olympics.

Why is proper breathing so important when doing a flip turn?

Go online to watch videos of people performing flip turns. Then watch some videos of people performing open turns, where they touch the wall with their hand before turning around. How can you tell that the flip turn is more effective?

Look online for tips on how to do a flip turn. Why do you think beginning swimmers have such a hard time with it?

LEARN MORE

FURTHER READING

Dzidrums, Christine. *Missy Franklin: Swimming Sensation*. Whittier, CA: Creative Media, 2013.

Hyduk, Vallery. *Swim to Win*. Toronto: James Lorimer & Company Ltd., 2011.

Torsiello, David. *Michael Phelps: Swimming for Olympic Gold*. Berkeley Heights, NJ: Enslow Publishers, 2009.

WEB SITES

Livestrong.com—The History of Swimming for Kids
www.livestrong.com/article/383078-the-history-of-swimming-for-kids/
Read about swimming from ancient times to today.

Online Swim Trainer—Beginner's Guide to the Perfect Flip Turn
www.onlineswimtrainer.com/tips/beginner-flip-turn/
Find step-by-step directions on how to do a flip turn, along with videos.

Swimmingpool.com—Games & Safety: Fun Facts
www.swimmingpool.com/games-safety/pool-fun/fun-facts
Read trivia and facts about swimming.

GLOSSARY

butterfly (BUHT-ur-flye) a difficult swimming stroke where both arms arch above the water, and the swimmer does a dolphin kick

conventional (kuhn-VEN-shuh-nuhl) common or traditional

drag (DRAG) a force which slows down the movement of an object

efficient (i-FISH-uhnt) working very well and not wasting time or energy

energy (EN-ur-jee) the ability of something to do work

momentum (moh-MEN-tuhm) the property that a moving object has because of its mass and its motion

rotation (roh-TAY-shun) twist, turn

somersault (SUHM-ur-sawlt) a movement made forward or backward in which the body rolls end over end in a complete turn

streamlined (STREEM-lined) designed or shaped to minimize resistance to water or air

velocity (vuh-LAH-si-tee) rate of speed in a particular direction

INDEX

[21ST CENTURY SKILLS LIBRARY]

Deadpool #28,
Spider-Man/Deadpool #15 and
Deadpool & the Mercs for Money #9
connecting covers

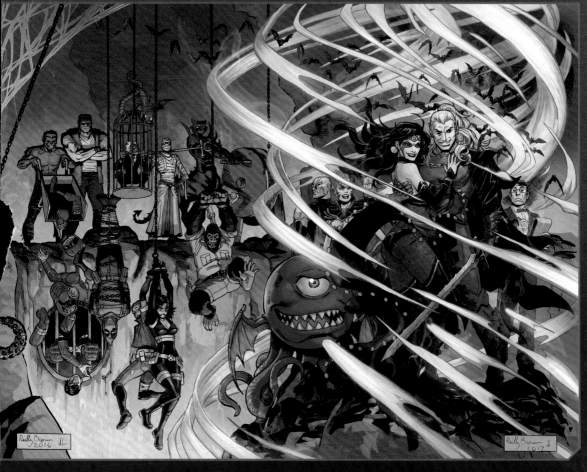

Deadpool #28
Venomized variant by
DAVID LOPEZ

Spider-Man/Deadpool #15
Venomized variant by
DAVID WILLIAMS
& JORDAN BOYD